Meet the Artist

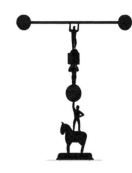

Illustrated by

Rose Blake

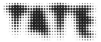

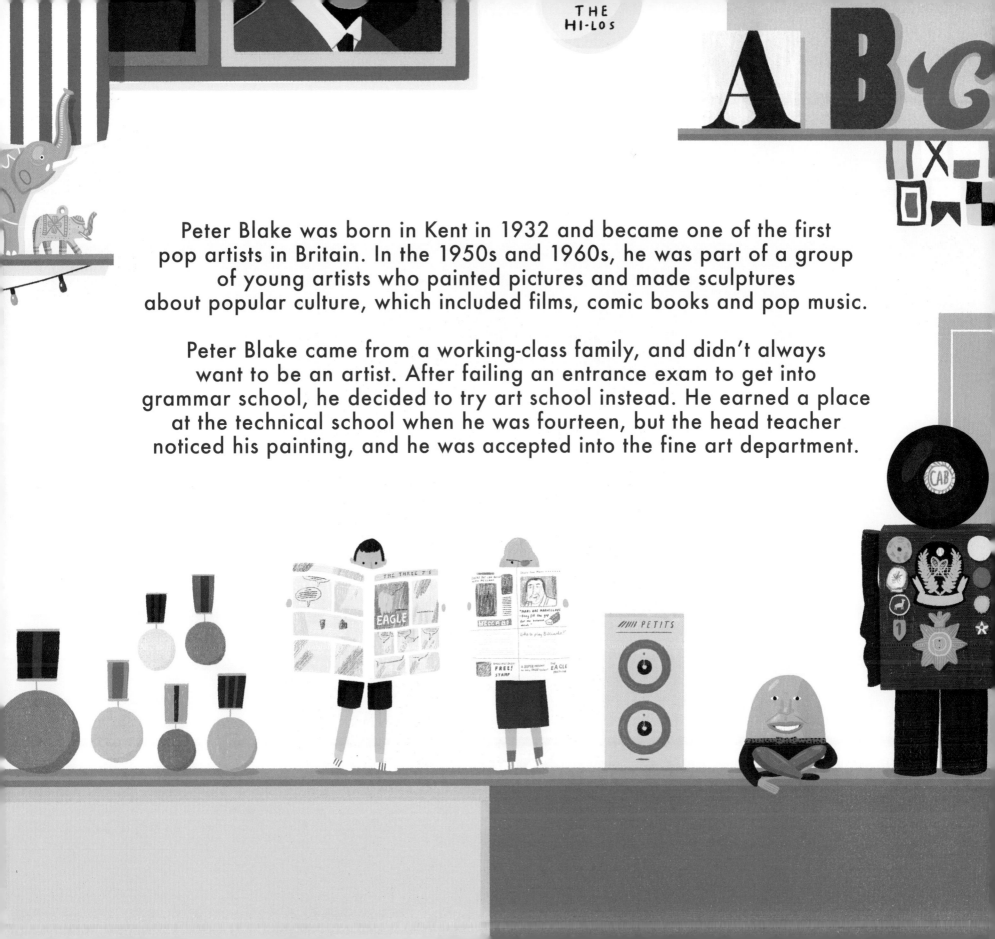

Peter Blake was born in Kent in 1932 and became one of the first pop artists in Britain. In the 1950s and 1960s, he was part of a group of young artists who painted pictures and made sculptures about popular culture, which included films, comic books and pop music.

Peter Blake came from a working-class family, and didn't always want to be an artist. After failing an entrance exam to get into grammar school, he decided to try art school instead. He earned a place at the technical school when he was fourteen, but the head teacher noticed his painting, and he was accepted into the fine art department.

At the beginning of his career, Blake was inspired by American culture. After the Second World War, life in Britain was very grey and he loved dreaming of glamorous American clothes, films and music.

In this self-portrait, Blake is standing in his gloomy back garden wearing denim jeans and a jacket with lots of badges. Look at the painting carefully. What things do you think he was interested in?

ADLAI IS OK

DO A GOOD TURN DAILY

I LIKE Florello!

TEMPERANCE 7

ELVIS

LODGE

Draw yourself here in a special outfit.
Decorate these badges by drawing your favourite things in them.

Think about your favourite pop stars, gadgets, books, TV shows and films.

Like many other children living in London during the Second World War,
Blake was evacuated to safety in the countryside. This meant that he didn't have
many toys growing up, so to make up for it he collected lots of toys as an adult!

In this artwork, he recreated the window of a toyshop using the toys from his collection.
Can you spot the toys in the window?
There is an aeroplane, a clown mask, a paintbrush and a red train.

Fill this toyshop window with drawings of your favourite toys.

In the 1950s, artists in England and America started making pop art.
Pop is short for 'popular' and celebrates popular culture.

Pop artists made pictures about music, comic books, TV programmes and food.

Pop art was colourful, bold and inspired by the things that the artists loved the most.

3

The words below describe things that are often used as images in pop art.
Add pictures from magazines or photographs, or draw your own images to fill in the grid.

A star	A heart	A drink	A flag
A pop star	A special book	Your initials	A rainbow
A bullseye target	Your favourite word	A cartoon character	A number
A superhero	A fast car	Your favourite food	Your pet

This painting is called *On the Balcony*. Blake has included
twenty-seven images inside his painting that are all about being on a balcony.

Can you spot them all? Which is your favourite? Why?

When you look closely at a painting, you notice details that you might otherwise miss! Here is a close-up of the table from the painting on the previous page. What new details can you spot?

Music is a big inspiration in Blake's work. He loves listening to loud rock and roll and jazz while painting in his studio.

He made the artwork opposite about one of his favourite songs, called 'Got a Girl'.

The lyrics of the song include the names of all the pop stars at the top of the picture. In the top left, Blake added the actual record so you could listen to the song while looking at the picture.

Artist's Advice
I wanted to make an art that was the equivalent of pop music.

Listen to your favourite song and draw pictures of the lyrics in the boxes above.

One of Blake's most famous artworks is the album cover for
Sgt. Pepper's Lonely Hearts Club Band by The Beatles.

Blake asked each member of The Beatles to write a list of their favourite people,
then he made a life-size crowd of the people cut out from cardboard.

Blake then asked The Beatles to stand in the middle, wearing colourful suits,
and a photographer took a picture of the scene.

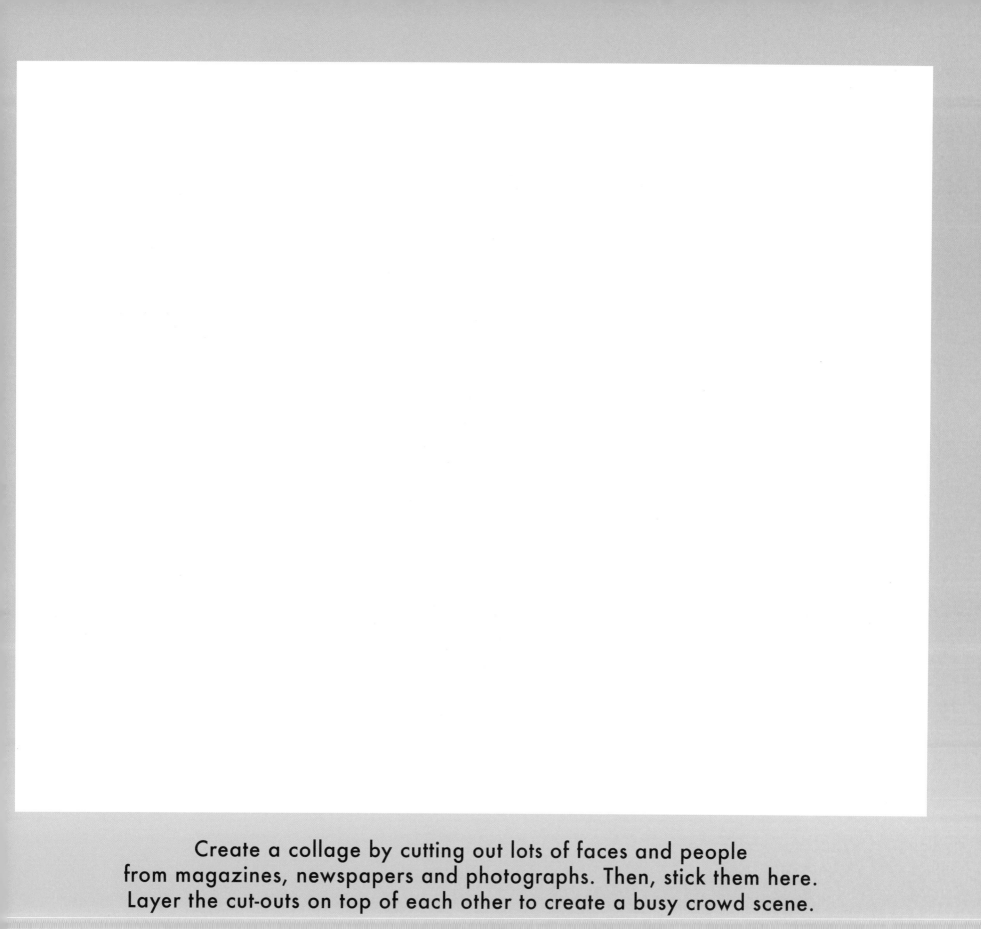

Create a collage by cutting out lots of faces and people
from magazines, newspapers and photographs. Then, stick them here.
Layer the cut-outs on top of each other to create a busy crowd scene.

Blake loves books and he often uses them as inspiration for his paintings and illustrations. One of his favourite books is *Alice's Adventures in Wonderland* by Lewis Carroll.

In the book, Alice joins the Mad Hatter, the March Hare and the Dormouse for an exciting tea party.

Draw lots of tasty food and drinks to add to this tea party. Don't forget to include yourself and your friends at the table.

Blake uses lots of different paintbrush techniques when creating his paintings.
Different brushstrokes help artists to create different textures
in their paintings, such as skin, fabrics, furs and objects.
The image above shows the different kinds of brushstrokes you can try.

Use the techniques you've learnt to paint the things below:

A rose	Tree bark	A cat
A hand	A marble	A book
A tornado	A sheep	A raindrop

Collage is a great way to create interesting pictures, all you need is a pencil, different types of paper, scissors and glue! Once you have these items, use your pencil to draw shapes on the different types of paper.

CHART

E

Then, carefully cut out the shapes. Next, glue the shapes to the page below to create your collage. Layer the pieces of paper to create different shapes and textures. Let your imagination go wild!

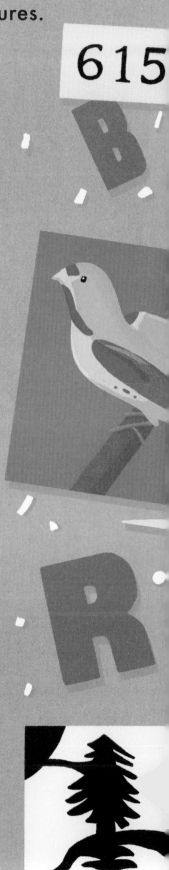

Create a collage on the following page using lots of things that begin with the first letter of your name.

For example, if your name was Rose, you would find pictures of things starting with the letter 'R'.

You might use a robot, a rat, a radiator, a raspberry or a rubber.

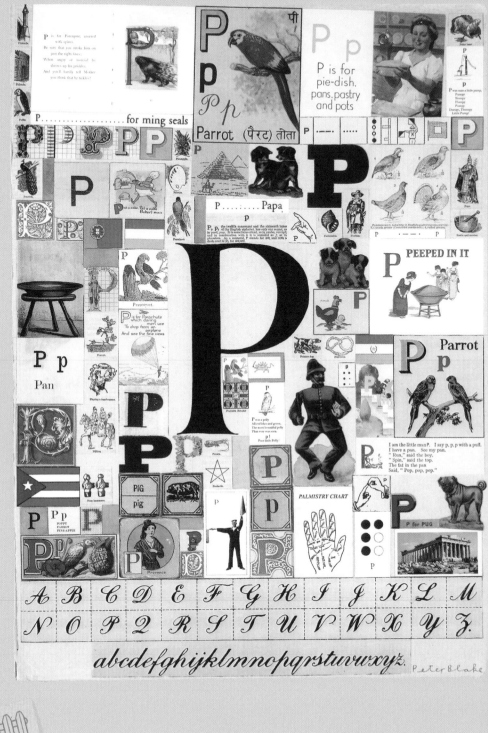

Arrange the things before sticking them down with glue or tape.
Making a collage is just like doing a jigsaw puzzle!

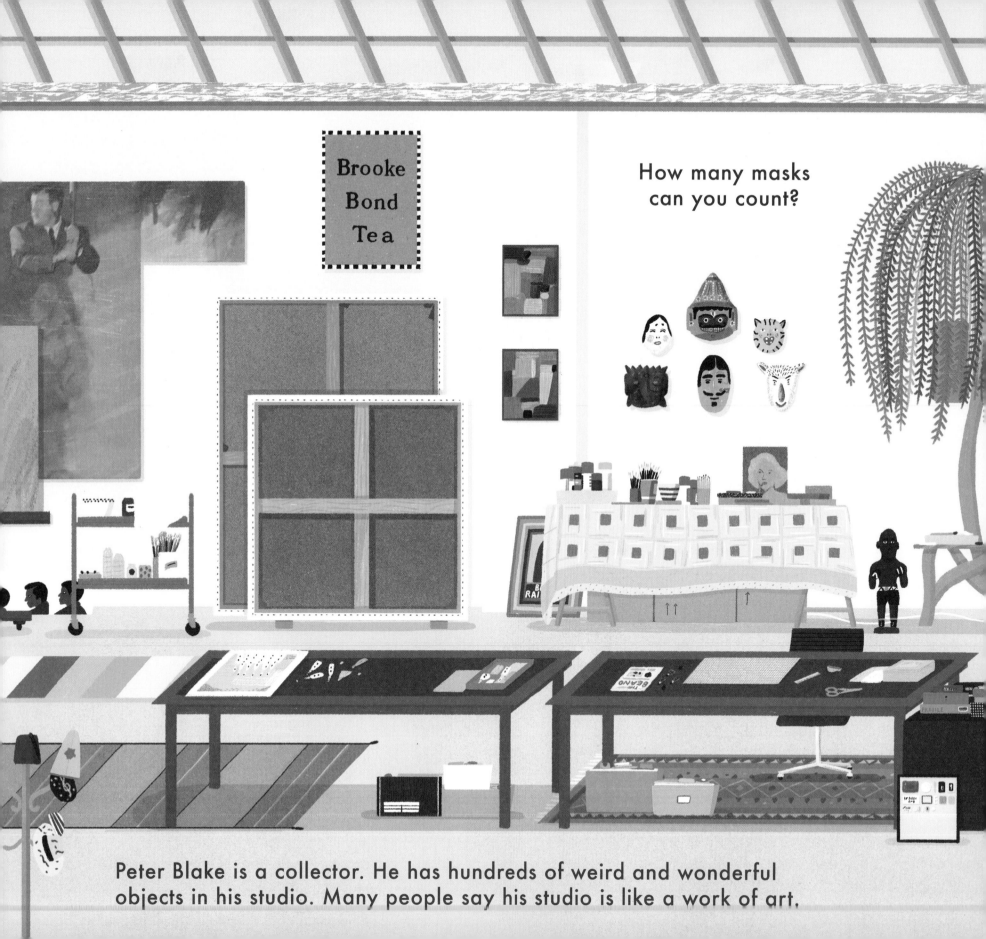

Brooke Bond Tea

How many masks can you count?

Peter Blake is a collector. He has hundreds of weird and wonderful objects in his studio. Many people say his studio is like a work of art.

What can you see
on the shelves?

What would you
like to collect?

Use collage, drawings and photographs to curate your own museum here. You can pick all your favourite things.

Blake has added a few of his elephants to start you off!

You'll often see the objects Blake has collected appearing in his artworks.

In this image, he has put lots of black-and-white objects together and arranged them in a grid.

Museum of Black & White. 8.   Peter Blake. 2010.

Collect twenty objects that are all the same colour and arrange them in a square.
Take a photo of the objects using a camera or a phone, then stick the photo here.

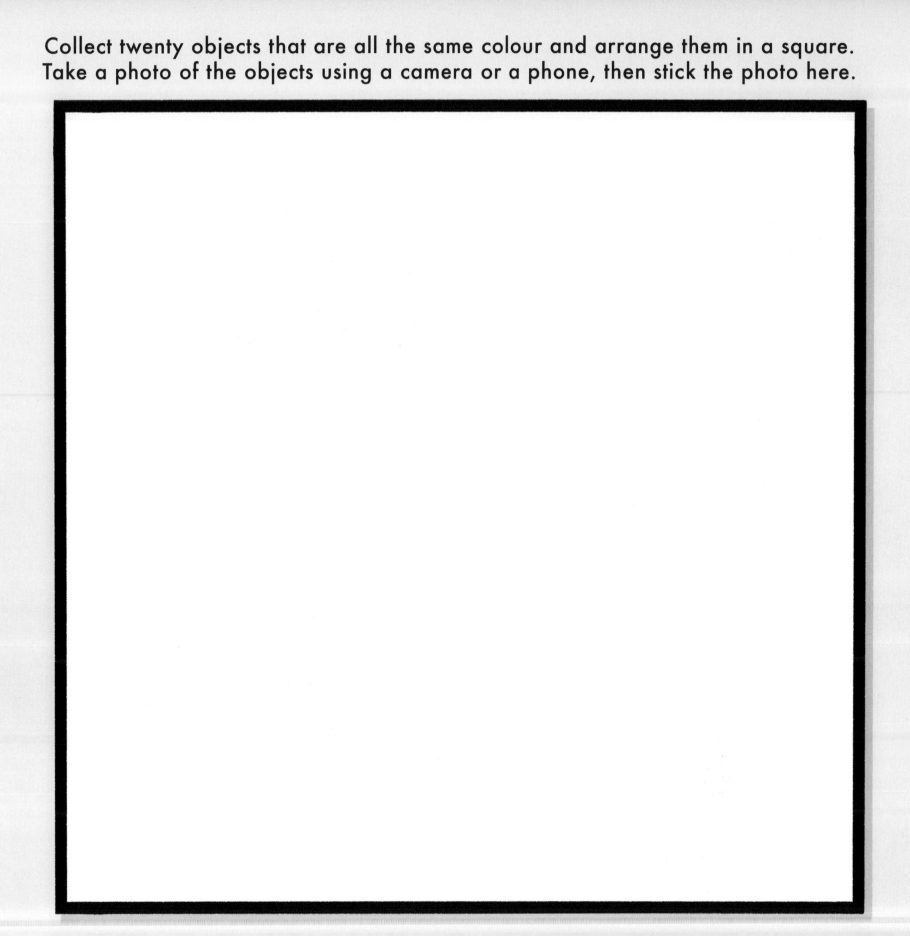

Page 4
Peter Blake
Self-Portrait with Badges
1961
Oil paint on board
179.2 x 126.5 cm
Tate

Page 6
Peter Blake
The Toy Shop
1962
Wood, glass, paper, plastic,
fabric and other materials
156.8 x 194 x 34 cm
Tate

Page 8
Peter Blake
Sources of Pop Art I
2000
Silkscreen print (edition of 50)
30.7 x 30.7 cm

Page 10
Peter Blake
On the Balcony
1955–7
Oil paint on canvas
132.4 x 101.7 cm
Tate

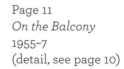

Page 11
On the Balcony
1955–7
(detail, see page 10)

Page 13
Peter Blake
Got a Girl
1960–1
Oil paint, wood, photo-collage, record
94 x 154.9 cm
Whitworth Art Gallery

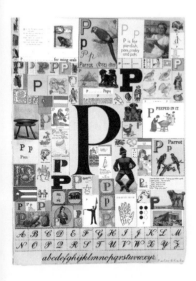

Page 22
Peter Blake
An Alphabet: P
2009
Collage
52 x 37 cm

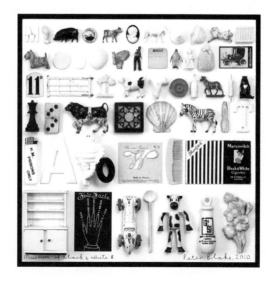

Page 28
Peter Blake
Museum of Black & White 8
(in homage to Mark Dion)
2010
Collage with found objects
42.5 x 42.5 cm

With special thanks to Chrissy

First published 2019 by order of the Tate Trustees
by Tate Publishing, a division of Tate Enterprises Ltd,
Millbank, London SW1P 4RG
www.tate.org.uk/publishing

A catalogue record for this book is available from the British Library

ISBN 978 1 84976 625 8

Distributed in the United States and Canada by ABRAMS, New York
Library of Congress Control Number applied for

Colour reproduction by DL Imaging, London
Printed in China by Toppan Leefung Printing Ltd.

Measurements of artworks are given in centimetres, height before width